POMPEII

MONUMENTS
PAST AND PRESENT

Text by **A. DE FRANCISCIS** with updating revision by **I. BRAGANTINI**
Drawings and reconstructions: Vision s.r.l.
Layout: U.Ulivieri

PAST & PRESENT®

ISBN 88- 8162-018-9

Printed in Italy by Tipolitografica CS - Padova

POMPEI, ITS LIFE AND HISTORY

Pompeii stands on a lava spur running out into the plain from the slopes of Vesuvius, a short distance from the sea and from the river Sarno. The site was well suited for human settlement, of an agricultural and commercial character, and was probably already inhabited from an early date, when Campania was still occupied by the Oscans. In early historical times the existence of a temple of Greek type dating from the middle of the 6th century B.C. attests the context of the relations with the neighbouring greek colonies became very complex, in particular with Cuma, as well as with the Etruscan world, which on several occasions clashed with the Greeks in an attempt to oust them from the control of this region. Pompeii was involved in the invasion and subsequent domination of Campania by the Samnites (about 424 B.C.), and from this moment on we are better informed about the lay-out and development of the city. It was, however, only a small place, and mentions of it in the history of the following centuries are correspondingly few.

During the Samnite wars it repelled an attack by a Roman naval raiding party, but with the establishment of peace it entered the Roman orbit as an allied city, an alliance to which it remained faithful even during the dark days of the Carthaginian invasion under Hannibal. Throughout this period Pompeii kept its commercial independence, its own magistrates and language; then, in the Social war, it became involved on the side of the Italic allies and in 89 B.C. it was besieged, stormed and subjected by Sulla. In 80 it was settled as a Roman colony under the name of *Colonia Cornelia Veneria Pompeiorum.* Henceforth its history is part of the larger picture of Roman history. The only local episode of note, mentioned by Tacitus, is a riot in the amphitheatre between the inhabitants of Pompeii and Nuceria (A.D. 59), which led to the suspension of all spectacles for a period of ten years.

Pompeii was badly damaged by the earthquake which hit Campania in A.D. 62 and the damage had not all been repaired when, in 79, an eruption of Vesuvius killed many of the inhabitants and buried the whole city beneath a rain of ash and cinders. A graphic description of the disaster is given in two letters by Pliny the Younger to Tacitus, describing among other things the rescue work undertaken by his uncle, Pliny the Elder, who was at the time commander of the Roman fleet at Misenum and who paid for his generous initiative with his life.

Pompeii never rose from its ruins and the site was virtually abandoned. The first signs of the buried city came to light between 1594 and 1600, when the architect Domenico Fontana cut a channel for the waters of the river Sarno; but on that occasion the exploration was not followed up. Then, in 1748, regular excavations were started by the king of Naples, Charles of Bourbon, and they have continued without a break ever since. During this long time methods of excavations have of course changed. At first the search was only for sculpture, paintings, mosaics and other objects of artistic interest or curiosity, and the ruins themselves were often reburied. With time, however, thanks to a steady improvement of excavation methods and an in-

Sign Board with Mercury emerging from his Temple and painted inscriptions for elections

creasing interest in the vestiges of the past, the remains were systematically explored and studied in all their manifold aspects, and every efforts was made to preserve and to restore them.

The object of the more recent excavations has been to present the houses and streets of Pompeii as they were, and to afford the visitor as complete a vision as possible of an ancient city. Mention may be made of the technique introduced by the great archaeologist, Giuseppe Fiorelli, whereby the shapes of buried organic features (human bodies, trees, wooden objects) are recovered by pouring plaster into the impressions left by their dissolution. Thanks to the exceptional circumstances of the burial of Pompeii (and of course of Herculaneum), where life suddenly came to an end in the space of two days, the excavator car reap a rich harvest, not only of the sort of remains which one can find in any part of the ancient world, but also of all sorts of objects, furniture and other items of daily life which elsewhere are apt to be scattered and destroyed. Here for example one can study in a wealth of varied examples the development of the Italic and Roman house and of its painted decoration from the 2nd century B.C. to the 1st century A.D.

The wall-paintings can be classified according to their style into four main groups, a classification which is based on decorative systems that can be dated within certain limits, and which is valid also for other archaeological sites that are less well documented. Another valuable contribution to knowledge is that which the scratched and painted inscriptions of Pompeii make to the history of manners, institutions and the spoken language of the Roman world in the 1st century A.D.

In the final phase of the city, as one sees it today, it was surrounded by walls with defensive towers and gates. There were two main streets running east and west (*decumani*), the Via di Nola and the Via dell'Abbondanza, and one north and south (*cardo*), the Via di Stabia. The other roads mostly ran parallel to these. The city-centre, the Forum, lay towards the south-west, with other centres of public life around the Triangular Forum and the Amphitheatre.

House of the Vettii:
Cupids as Goldsmiths

POMPEII

VILLA DEI MISTERI

VIA DI NOLA

PORTA DI NOLA

VIA DELL'ABBONDANZA

VIA DI MERCURIO

VIA DI STABIA

PORTA VESUVIO

REGIO IV

PORTA DI SARNO

REGIO V

REGIO III

REGIO II

VIA DEI SEPOLCRI

PORTA ERCOLANO

REGIO VI

REGIO IX

REGIO VII

VICOLO DI MERCURIO

VIA DELLA FORTUNA

REGIO I

PORTA DI NOCERA

REGIO VIII

PORTA DI STABIA

PORTA MARINA

ANTIQUARIUM

0   100   500 m.

■■■■ reconstructed monuments

░░░░ described monuments

THE MONUMENTS OF POMPEI

Porta Marina (Sea Gate)

1 PORTA MARINA AND VILLA SUBURBANA

The Porta Marina dates from the 2nd century B.C. and is one of the best preserved of the several gates that open through the city-walls of Pompeii. It faces towards the sea, whence its name; and although the road through it is rather too steep for comfort, it affords the most direct link between the hill on which Pompeii stands and the coastal plain. Inside the gate the road, under the name of the Via Marina, passes between the Temple of Venus, the Basilica and the Temple of Apollo and leads straight to the city-centre, the Forum. The gate is spanned by a single barrel vault, within which are two passage-ways: that on the left, up steps, for foot passengers, that on the right, somewhat less steep, for pack-animals; it was probably too steep for vehicles. The passages were closed by double doors. With the establishment of peace, under Augustus, the walls lost their military purpose and a villa was built up against the outer face, to the right of the Gate. The part so far excavated includes a long portico wing opening on to a dining hall with Third Style paintings and a group of other rooms. In front of it, spreading over the line of the early road leading up to the Gate, was a large garden.

2 TEMPLE OF VENUS

Dominating the plain below, and formerly surrounded by a wall of reticulate masonry, is the sacred precinct of Venus, the protecting divinity of Pompeii. In the middle is the temple podium, and here and there are traces of the earlier buildings that were demolished to make way for the sanctuary. The temple was adorned with marble, and the character of the surviving remains indicates a considerable degree of opulence; but it was badly damaged in the earthquake of 62, and it was still in ruins when it was overwhelmed by the eruption.

3 THE FORUM (REG. VII)

Along the south side were three large halls, richly decorated in marble, no doubt intended to serve the administrative life of Pompeii. In them we can recognize the seat of the *duoviri* and of the *aediles*, the two principal magistracies, and that of the *ordo decurionum*, corresponding to our own city council.

On the west there is the main entrance of the Basilica; then, across the Via Marina and opening off it, with one side towards the Forum, the Temple of Apollo; and finally a group of buildings connected with the storage and sales of basic foodstuffs such as cereals and vegetables. It comprises the *mensa ponderaria*, the official units of measure, and a small market and storerooms.

At the north end of the piazza stands the Temple of Jupiter, picturesquely flanked by two honorary arches. This was the main city temple, built in the Samnite period and later transformed into a *Capitolium*, to house the Capitoline triad of Jupiter, Juno and Minerva. Within the lofty podium are rooms which served to house the city-treasury (*aerarium*) and the ex-voto offerings (*favissae*); a flight of steps led up to the temple proper, which had a deep Corinthian porch and a *cella* (shrine) flanked by columns. At the time of the eruption it was not yet in use after the damage incurred in the earthquake.

THE FORUM AND THE CAPITOLIUM

The centre of an ancient city was a large open space, the Forum. Around it stood the main public buildings, both civil and religious, and it was adorned with numerous monuments, serving as a setting for important ceremonial occasions and frequently also for spectacles and games. The Forum of Pompeii still preserves substantially its ancient aspect of a rectangular piazza, 124 ft. x 482 ft., running north and south, with a paving of travertine slabs and surrounded on three sides by porticoes. The porticoes are not all alike. Along the south side are parts of the original colonnade of the Samnite period, whereas the two storeys of travertine colonnades along the other two sides represent a reconstruction that was begun during the Empire, but never completed; and some buildings have

The Forum: reconstruction

porticoes of their own in front of them. Barriers prevented traffic from entering from the adjoining streets. Within the piazza stood the *suggestum* (a platform for orators) and statues erected in honour of members of the Imperial family and distinguished local citizens; but of these only the bases remain.

The Forum:
detail of the eastern portico

4 THE TEMPLE OF APOLLO (REG. VII)

The earliest traces of cult, revealed in deep excavations, go back to the 6th century B.C., but the present lay-out is of the Samnite period, with various alterations in Roman times. The precinct consists of an enclosing wall with porticoes on three sides, of which the columns were originally Ionic, carrying a Doric frieze of metopes and triglyphs. After the earthquake of 62 a facing of stucco, now destroyed, transformed the columns into Corinthian, and the frieze became continuous and was decorated with motives associated with the cult of Apollo.

To this period belong also the Fourth Style wall-paintings, with scenes from the Trojan cycle; and in front of the portico there were herms of Mercury and Maia and statues of divinities, including Apollo, Diana, Hermaphrodite and Venus. In the Augustan period the duoviri M. Holconius Rufus and

The Temple of Apollo: reconstruction

C. Egnatius Postumus for 300 sesterces bought up the rights of the proprietor whose house overlooked the sanctuary from the west, raising the outer wall on this side to roof height.

The temple stood on a podium with steps in front, and inside the cella was the cult statue and a stone *omphalo*s, attribute of Apollo. The pavement was the work of the quaestor Ovius Campanus.

The altar, of Republican date and erected by the quattuorviri on the order of the decurions, stood in the open space in front of the temple; and beside the steps stood a column, placed there by the duoviri, L. Sepanius and M. Herennius, bearing a dedicatory inscription and carrying a sundial. It is not unlikely that the cult of Apollo was in some way associated in this temple with that also of the emperor Augustus, who had a special devotion for the god under whose protection he had won the battle of Actium in 31 B.C. against Antony and Cleopatra.

Bronze Statue of Apollo

5 THE BASILICA (REG. VII)

The Basilica lies at the south-west corner of the Forum, behind the portico. The five doors of the entrance are preceded by a vestibule, the *chalcidicum*, and there are two lesser entrances in the long sides (but that on the southern side, facing the houses of Regio VIII, was opened subsequently). Inside there is a colonnade of brick running round all four sides, of which only the lower part survives, and a responding line of two orders of half-columns along the walls. The latter are decorated in the Pompeian First Style, and at the far end stands the *tribunal,* a tall platform with a double order of superimposed columns but the pediment is the result of a mistaken restoration carried out in the twenties (1928-30). The building as a whole dates from the last decades of the 2nd century B.C., and there is an inscription of 78 B.C. scratched on one of the walls. It was wrecked by the earthquake of 62, and there is no sign

The Basilica:
reconstruction of the interior

of any restoration before the final catastrophe. The reconstruction that is proposed herein shows a building with a double sloping roof, that receives light from the upper floor intercolumn.

Certainly the Basilica and the Forum together constituted the centre of life and activity of the ancient city, the more so in view of the manifold mercantile interests of Pompeii. For the merchant or banker conducting affairs, for the idler with time on his hands, for the quick-witted anxious to put his leisure to good account, for all these this was the natural place of resort.

Plan of the Forum

BUILDINGS OF THE FORUM

6 THE COMITIUM. Another group of public buildings stood along the east side of the Forum. Starting at the south end there is the *Comitium*, with doors both from the street and from the Forum. Its function was as a place of meeting for the popular election of the magistrates.

7 THE EUMACHIA BUILDING, so-called after the priestess who, in the 1st century A.D., dedicated it in her own name and that of her son, Numistrius Fronto to *Concordia Augusta* and *Pietas*. This was the seat of the guild of Fullers (*fullones*), dyers and cleaners, practising one of the most widespread of ancient crafts; it was also used for the storage and sale of stuffs. In front of it was a two-storeyed portico (*chalcidicum*) and a façade with a large marble doorway, decorated with acanthus scrollwork and flanked by four niches housing statues of Aeneas, Romulus, Augustus and Tibe-

Area of the Temple of Vespasian

rius, in imitation of the Forum of Augustus in Rome. The inner courtyard had a two storeyed portico and, behind the portico, a corridor lit by windows (*cryptoporticus*). In the apse at the end must have stood the statue of Concordia Augusta, and in the corridor behind it was found the statue of Eumachia. There is a secondary entrance from the Via dell'Abbondanza.

8 THE so-called TEMPLE OF VESPASIAN, in front of which stands a handsome marble altar depicting a sacrificial scene, and around it, delimited by an outer wall and fronted by a portico, the sacred precinct (*templum*).

9 THE so-called SHRINE OF THE LARES, a spacious building once richly decorated with sculpture and marble ornament. The rear wall breaks out into an apse and in the middle stands the sacrificial altar. Though stripped of all its superficial detail, the plan is unusual and interesting. There is good reason to believe that it served as the place of worship for the *Lares publici*, the city's protecting divinities.

10 THE MACELLUM, a large market, the present plan of which goes back to the first century of the Empire. It consists of an open central area around which, opening partly inwards and partly outwards towards the street, were rows of shops. In the centre stood a circular building (*tholos*) with columns and a pool of water, and at the back a small shrine devoted to the Imperial cult, in which probably stood statues of the emperor and members of his family. (Two of these were found and are now in the Museum of Naples, but their identities are disputed).

*The Macellum:
detail of the portico*

11 THE TEMPLE OF FORTUNA AUGUSTA (REG. VII)

This dates from the closing years of the 1st century B.C. and was built, at his own expense and on his own land, by one M. Tullius, who had filled numerous public offices at Pompeii - three times duovir, quinquennalis, augur and military tribune by popular election. It was badly damaged in the earthquake of 62, and was still being rebuilt at the time of the eruption. By that date it seems already to have been for a some time in a state of decline. The flight of steps in front is interrupted by a platform at the foot, on which stood the altar (probably that reused in Flavian times for the nearby temple of Vespasian), and it was enclosed within a railing. The deep porch was carried on marble Corinthian columns and behind it the cella too was cased in marble; in the middle of the rear wall was an aedicula with colonnettes and an inscribed architrave recording the act of foundation, and along the side walls were niches for statues, two of which have survived. The temple was dedicated to Fortuna Augusta, a cult established in A.D. 3 in honour of Augustus in his capacity as "Father of his Country", and is an indication of the progressive divinization of the emperor which was already taking place under the influence of the Hellenistic courts, and which was to become increasingly important as the Empire developed. The Pompeian cult was in the hands of the *Ministri Fortunae Augustae,* a religious college recorded in a number of inscriptions.

Each year, on the instructions of the duoviri and aediles, the *Ministri* deposited a small statue (*signum*) in the temple. It occupied a central position, a short distance from the Forum, at the cross-roads between a street leading from the Forum and the Via di Nola. To the south of it ran a handsome portico with shops opening off it; across the street were the Forum Baths; and over the cross-roads to the north there was a honorary arch, on which stood a bronze statue, fragments of which have been recovered.

12 THE FORUM BATHS

The Forum Baths are of Sullan date and were built by the duovir L. Caesius and the aediles C.Occius and L. Niremius.

As was regular practice in the baths of this period, there were separate sections for men and women. The former consisted of a changing room (*apodyterium*); a circular *frigidarium*; a *tepidarium*, in which one can see still in place the brazier, together with the seating presented by M. Nigidius

The Temple of the Fortuna Augusta:
reconstruction

Vascula; and a *calidarium* of which the basin was installed in A.D. 3-4, by Cn. Melissius Aper and M. Statius Rufus.

The women's wing was similarly organized, except that the *frigidarium* was connected with the *apodyterium.* The furnace (*praefurnium*) lay between the two wings, the hot air circulating through a system of double walls (*concameratio*) and of paving raised on *suspensurae.* The rooms were elegantly decorated in painted stucco, with mythological scenes, foliate ornament and caryatid figures. A porticoed palestra occupied a part of the site.

13 THE HOUSE OF THE TRAGIC POET

A typical example of a Pompeian house with tuscan atrium and peristyle, and an upper storey, accessible from the atrium. It is richly and eleganted decorated with painting and mosaics. In the entrance is a pavement depicting a dog on a chain and the words *cave canem* ("beware of the dog"). The wall-paintings of the atrium were large pictures of mythological subjects, including Zeus and Hera, and Achilles and Briseis. Off the atrium opened the bedrooms and the *alae*, both well decorated, and in the centre of the rear wall the *tablinum*, in which were a small mosaic panel of theatrical actors and a picture of Admetus and Alcestis. A small portico occupies three sides of the peristyle. Here there was another well-known painting, the Sacrifice of Iphigenia, after Pheimantes (5th-

The Forum Baths: tepidarium

The Forum Baths: calidarium

4th century B.C.), and at the back a lararium.

Off the portico open three rooms, one of them a dining room decorated in the Fourth Style with other mythological subjects (Venus and Cupids, Ariadne Abandoned, Diana). Some of the paintings and the mosaic panel are in the Naples Museum.

14 THE HOUSE OF SALLUST (REG. VI)

A typical example of a Pompeian house of the Samnite period, built in squared tufa masonry, with a Tuscan atrium; the doors are taller than they are wide and taper gently upward. To this period also belongs the well-preserved First Style wall-decoration. Various additions were made during the first century of the Empire - a little peristyle with hexagonal columns; a courtyard garden (*viridarium*), and a bakery (*pistrinum*). A typical sign of the times and of the changing needs of the owners is the opening of two shops on either side of the main entrance.

House of the Tragic Poet:
Achilles and Briseis
(National Museum of Naples)

15 THE HERCULANEUM GATE

The ancient name of this was the *Porta Saliniensis* (Oscan "Veru Sarinu"), leaning as it did to the village (*pagus* or *vicus*) of the *Salinienses*, whose inhabitants worked in the salt-pans. It also served the road to Herculaneum, whence the modern name. It stands at the end of the Via Consolare, and in its present form, with three arches, a broad opening in the centre for vehicles and two smaller ones for foot-passengers, it represents the form which it assumed during the Roman period, after it had lost all defensive function.

For the city's defences in their various stages of development one must turn instead to the various traces of the fortifications of Pompei, of which the most ancient phases go back to the 6th century B.C. During the 5th century over the same line of the pre-existing wall, a lime-stone fortification was raised. The external curtain wall was built the Samnite period (2nd century B.C.); the wall of concreted rubble masonry and the towers can be dated to the following century and are slightly earlier the Social wars and the siege by the Romans.

16 THE STREET OF THE TOMBS (Via delle Tombe)

Outside the Herculaneum Gate lies the Street of the Tombs. Not yet completely excavated, it is one of the most suggestive corners of Pompeii, sloping gently down the hillside towards the plain and the sea and flanked of both sides, as was customary in the classical world, by funerary monuments, with here and there also the entries to suburban villas, and porticoes with shops. On the left-hand side the most interesting monuments are the "Tomb of the Garlands", of Republican date, so-called from the ornament of its architrave; and the "Tomb of the Blue Vase", from the vase of white-on-blue cameo-glass with cupids gathering grapes that was found in it and is now in the Naples museum. On the same side lies the entrance to the " Villa of the Mosaic Columns", on the site of an earlier Samnite cemetery (3rd century B.C.); in the garden were found a large fountain faced with glass paste and shells and, similarly ornamented, the four columns of a pergola (now in the Naples Museum) after which it is named. Next, after a row of shops, the road forks. Beyond the fork, on the left, lies the "Villa of Diomede", followed by a group of monuments of noble citizens: of Umbricius Scaurus, with gladiatorial scenes in stucco; of Calventius Quietus; of Saturninus, in the form of a banqueting couch; of Munatius Faustus; and various funerary precincts, marble ornaments (notable among them that erected on the tomb of Munatius Faustus by his wife, Naevoleia Tyche, with representations of a funeral ceremony and a ship) and inscriptions; and fi-

The Street of the Tombs

The Herculaneum Gate:
reconstruction

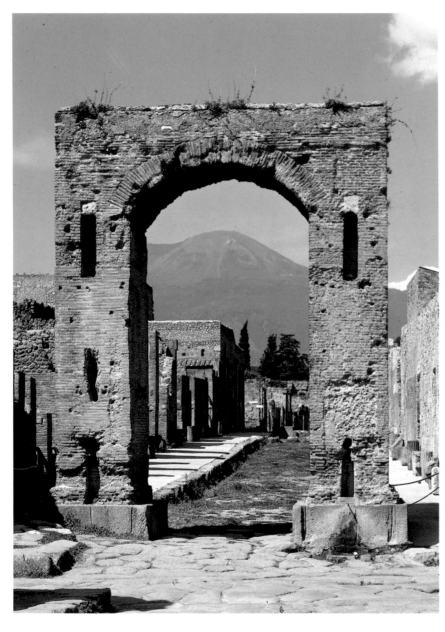

North-east corner of the Forum: Arch of Caligula and Via di Mercurio

nally the large and wealthy "Villa of Cicero", no longer visible because reburied soon after its discovery in 1763. Near the Herculaneum Gate there is another fine group of funerary monuments, among them that of the Istacidii family in the form of a temple on a podium, and that of the priestess Mamia, in the form of an exedra.

17 THE HOUSE OF MELEAGER (REG. VI)

From the Via di Mercurio one enters into this house, which can be called termed a luxury house, going back to the Samnite period but refurbished and redecorated in the 1st century A.D. with paintings and stuccoes in the fashionable Fourth Style. A large pool with marble ornaments occupies the centre of the graceful peristyle, and opening off the east portico a hall with a colonnade round the inner walls (a so-called *oecus corinthius*). A feature

House of Meleager: peristyle

*House of the Large Fountain:
fountain covered with mosaic*

unusual for the period is the use of arches, instead of the familiar flat architrave, in this colonnade.

18 THE HOUSE OF THE LARGE FOUNTAIN (REG. VI)

This house takes its name from an unusual feature of its garden, namely a fountain in the shape of a niche faced with polychrome glass-paste mosaic, from which water pours into a basin.

Masks and statuettes add to the wealth of ornament. A feature worthy of note is the main door into the house, which is built of fine, squared tufa masonry, and opens onto via di Mercurio.

19 THE HOUSE OF THE FAUN (REG. VI)

The largest and finest house in Pompeii, remarkable alike for the dignity of its architecture, for the sober refinement of its First-Style wall-decoration, in squares of polished stucco imitating slabs of variegated marble, and for the high quality of its mosaics (now in the Naples Museum). The pavement in front of the entrance bears the greeting, *have*; within it, high in the walls, are two lararia; and beyond it the Tuscan atrium, with a bronze statuette of a dancing Faun, a fine Hellenistic original of the 3rd-2nd century B.C., in the impluvium. Off the atrium open the bedrooms and, at the far end, the tablinum and two dining rooms, one for winter use with a mosaic of marine creatures, and one for autumn with Dionysus riding a panther. To the right of the atrium there is another living quarters with its own atrium of which the roof is supported on four columns (a "tetrastyle atrium"). Beyond lies the first peristyle, with porticoes on Ionic columns and a fountain in the middle of the garden and, opening off one side, the service rooms (kitchen, bath, etc.); at the far end two more dining rooms, for spring and summer use, and a large hall, the pavement of which portrayed the Battle of Alexander, a magnificent composition based on the work of one of the great Greek artists (now in Naples Museum), and in the entrance, a Nilotic scene. Beyond this again lies a second and much larger peristyle, with a two-storeyed Doric portico. The house had an upper storey, of which little is left. The House of the Faun was built in the 2nd century B.C., in the Samnite period, and shows how strong Hellenistic influence was on the Italic architecture of the time. As for the majority of the houses in Pompei, the name of the family who lived in this house is not known, however it must have been one of the main families of Pompei's Samnite period. Therefore the fact should be stressed that their house kept on to the end of the life of the city its original decorations to which subtle allegorical meanings have been attributed), overcoming without apparent changes a period which certainly was of great turmoil to the life of Pompei, that is that of the social war of the resulting settling as a Roman colony in the year 80 B.C.

20 THE HOUSE OF THE VETTII (REG. VI)

A luxurious house, the plan of which varies somewhat from the traditional model. Whereas the House of the Faun embodies the Greek artistic tastes and culture of the Samnite nobility, this house represents the last phase of wealthy private building by the well-to-do commercial classes. Its owners, Aulus Vettius Conviva and Aulus Vettius

House of the Vettii:
frieze with Apollo and the omphalos

The House of the Faun:
reconstruction

Houses of the Vettii:
Cupids making perfumes

Restitutus, were merchants who undertook a radical restoration after the earthquake of 62. It is deservedly famous for the wealth of its Fourth Style decoration. Outside there are no *tabernae* or shops to strike a sordid commercial note. The entrance leads straight into a spacious atrium containing two strong-boxes (*arcae*); around the walls above the plinth runs a graceful frieze of cupids and spirits. Noteworthy among the several rooms opening off it is that on the left of the entrance, decorated with fantastic architecture, which frames small mythological pictures of Ariadne Abandoned and of Hero and Leander beneath a frieze of marine creatures; and in the next room others of Cyparissus and the wounded stag and of Pan and Eros. The peristyle is unusually elaborate and contains a garden that has been replanted with the same plants as in antiquity, forming a most attractive and suggestive setting for the fountains and sculpture that were found in it.

Three rooms open off the portico. The first is decorated with false architectural perspectives, seascape panels and pictures of figured subjects - Daedalus and Pasiphae, Ixion bound to his wheel, and Dionysus and Ariadne; the second with a similar setting and pictures of Hercules strangling the snakes, the Punishment of Pentheus and the Punishment of Dirce. The third is the great dining room, one of the most elegant decorative schemes yet found in the private houses of Pompeii. The field is red, divided by black panels simulating the arches of a loggia and decorated with Menads and satyrs. Below it runs a frieze of the most delicate, spirited workmanship, portraying cupids engaged in such varied

House of Vettii:
picture of Hercules strangling the snakes

Seascape panels

occupations as selling oil, chariot-racing, goldsmith's work, the vintage, selling wine, etc. The plinth too is subdivided, floral ornaments alternating with figured panels with Psyches, mythical scenes and pairs of lovers. The service rooms are grouped round a secondary atrium with an upper storey, and beyond this again lie the women's quarters (*gynaeceum*).

21 THE HOUSE OF THE GOLDEN CUPIDS (REG. VI)

The architectural plan of this house goes back to the Republican age, while the interior decoration can be dated to the Imperial era, around the mid of the 1st century A.D. The Tuscan atrium is simply planned, with a bedchamber on either side of the entrance and a tablinum at the far end; from the atrium and the tablinum doors lead into the peristyle beyond. The latter is displaced towards the left, and around it runs a handsome Doric portico with a garden in the centre and a variety of marble decorative sculpture - carved panels, *oscilla*, herms and theatrical masks. The living rooms lie along the wings of the portico, of which the west side is raised on several steps, like a stage-building with three doors and a crowning pediment. These arrangements suggest that the owner was interested in the theatre, and he seems also to have been interested in the cult of the Egyptian goddess Isis, of whom there is a shrine in the north portico. The name of the house derives from the small glass discs to be seen in the bed-chamber, framing figures of Cupids delicately incised on gold foil.

22 THE HOUSE OF L. CAECILIUS JUCUNDUS (REG. V)

The residence of one L. Caecilius Jucundus, who exercised the profession of a banker, at any rate until the year of the earthquake. In it were found the well-preserved and still legible business records of Jucundus, full of information about the economic life of the time and in particular about the financial operations of Jucundus himself. In the atrium were found a portrait herm of the banker's father, L. Caecilius Felix, one of the finest pieces recovered from the soil of Pompeii, and a lararium with two very interesting marble reliefs, naif but most expressive portrayals of a group of Pompeian buildings at the moment of the earthquake: on the one side the Forum, with the Temple of Jupiter and one of the honorary arches, and on the other the Vesuvius Gate, the walls and the *castellum aquae* which regulated the water supply. They are certainly ex-voto offerings (perhaps for the escape of Caecilius), and for all their failings as works of art they offer a vivid glimpse of the results of the earthquake.

23 THE HOUSE OF THE SILVER WEDDING (REG. V)

This house, one of the most luxurious in Pompeii, takes its name from the fact of its excavation in 1893, the year of the silver wedding of Umberto and Margherita di Savoia. Its last owner was a rich and influential citizen, L. Albucius Celsus. Built in the Samnite period, it underwent various alterations during the 1st century A.D. The noble atrium, with four tall columns supporting the roof, is decorated in the Second Style. The peristyle, a later addition, is of the type called Rhodian, in which one of the porticoes is taller than the others; its columns were subsequently faced in stucco, the lower parts smooth and the upper

Bustus of
L. Caecilius Felix

House of the
Silver Weddings:
yellow exedra

*House of the
Silver Weddings: the atrium*

*House of the Centenary:
lararium with the painting
of Bacchus and Vesuvius*

parts hexagonal. The decoration of the walls is of the Fourth Style. Adjoining it is a garden with an open-air triclinium. The elegant living rooms round the peristyle include one, which may have been a triclinium, of which the vault is carried on four columns (*oecus corinthius*) imitating red porphyry and the walls are decorated in the Second Style. There is also a large room with black walls, an exedra with a yellow bakground and a small bathing-suite. There was an upper storey to the rooms round the atrium.

24 THE HOUSE OF THE CENTENARY (REG. IX)

A very large house with two atria, the property of Aulus Rustius Verus, excavated in 1879 on the occasion of the eighteenth century from the burial of Pompei. The first atrium has a mosaic floor and is decorated in the Fourth Style with small panels of theatrical subjects; beyond it lie the tablinum and a peristyle, the front wing of which forms a loggia. In the garden was found the celebrated statuette of a satyr with a wine-skin; also a small mosaic-ornamented fountain. In the lararium of the second, smaller atrium was found the well-known painting of Bacchus and Vesuvius (now in the National Museum in Naples); it leads to a group of rooms finely decorated with mythological scenes and to a bath.

25 THE CENTRAL BATHS (REG. IX)

These occupy an entire block, at the junction of the Via di Nola and the Via di Stabia; built in brick, with much reuse of earlier materials, they were begun after the earthquake and were still unfinished when buried by the eruption. They represent a new, more strictly functional architectural scheme for this type of building, characterised by a more spacious and internally coherent lay-out, and by the use of windows for light and air, and of a single bathing-circuit, not divided into separate wings for men and women.

The main entrance is from the Via di Nola, leading into the palaestra courtyard, along the east side of which lie the bath-buildings proper; a changing-room (*apodyterium*) with a circular cold plunge, the *tepidarium*, and a *calidarium* with large niches in the walls of the long sides. A feature new to the traditional scheme is the *laconicum*, a circular room for the *sudatio*.

Descending the Via di Stabia and taking the first turning to the right (Reg. VII) one arrives at the *Pistrinum*.

26 PISTRINUM (bakery) (REG. VII)

The burial of Pompeii took place very rapidly. The inhabitants were barely able to escape carrying a few personal belongings; indeed, many failed to get away at all and died, victims of their own hesitation and of the poisonous fumes. The rain of ash and cinders was not, on the other hand, unduly destructive, and it preserved much of what it buried. The result has been to make Pompeii a dead city as fascinating to the visitor as it is instructive to the student of antiquity. Monuments and work of art are to be found on many archaeological sites; here we can see also the little things of daily life, almost perfectly preserved, and study the tangible traces of habits and customs that are recorded nowhere else, often not even in the classical texts. Examples of this are the shops, with their counters and containers for food stuffs and other goods; the workshops with their tools, the furniture still standing in place within the houses; and the inscriptions on the walls, which plunge us straight into the middle of a municipal electoral campaign.

This shows us all the essential elements of a *pistrinum* for making bread. In the middle are the mills. These are made of smooth basalt from Vesuvius or one of the other volcanic areas of Campania, and consist of a conical stone (*meta*) standing on circular masonry basis and, resting and rotating on the *meta*, a second, biconical stone hollowed out internally (*catillus*). A wooden framework with two horizontal arms allowed the latter to be turned either by human or by animal power, as one can understand from a painting in another bakery of the same region where a donkey, frequently used for this function, is shown behind Vesta on her Throne. The grain was poured into the upper hollow of the *catillus* and came out at the bottom ground into flour.

Pistrinum -Bakery: reconstruction

On the right are a series of long, low supports for the tables for preparing and stacking the loaves, and on the left was the oven for baking them. Next to the bakery was the shop. Many carbonized loaves have been found here and there in the excavations, giving us a good idea of the appearance of what was then, as now, the staple item of diet. A scratched inscription refers to the excellence of the Pompeian bread.

27 THE STABIAN BATHS (REG. VII)

These, the oldest public baths in Pompeii, take their name from their situation on the crossing of the Via Stabiana and the Via dell'Abbondanza. One can distinguish at least five building periods. Built in the Samnite period (2nd century B.C.), they were first restored and enlarged in the early years of the Roman colony, then again under the Empire, and finally once more after the earthquake. These last repairs were still unfinished, and the baths still out of action, at the moment of the eruption.

The Stabian Baths are an outstanding example of a type of building which was very common in the Roman world, and which with the centuries underwent many changes of structure and function.

The principal entrance, on the Via dell'Abbondanza, leads through a small, square vestibule into the *palaestra*, which was surrounded by porticoes on three sides. In the last restoration the tufa columns of these were faced with stucco, as also was the wall-surface of the fourth side, towards the west, which bears a scheme of fantasy architecture and figured panels in the manner of Fourth Style painting. The oldest part of the baths is the north wing, which includes a common hall for the *sudatio* and a series of small, dark rooms for individual bathers, each with a plunge-bath and heated by braziers. The main bath lies instead along the east wing and was as usual divided into sections for men and women. Adjoining the vestibule of the male section was the changing room (*apodyterium*) with seats and niches for one's clothes. From the vestibule one passed into the *frigidarium*, a circular room with four recesses and lit by an oculus in the cupola; and from the changing-room into the *tepidarium*, with its plunge-bath, and so into the *calidarium*, an apsed hall with a plunge for bathing and a circular basin for washing. The two latter rooms were damaged in the earthquake of 62 and had not yet been repaired at the time of the eruption. In both rooms the heating circulated in the space beneath the raised pavement and in the thickness of the wall; it came from a furnace between the two sections, above which one can see the seating for the three cylindrical hot-water boilers.

A separate entrance from the palaestra led down a corridor to the women's section. The *apodyterium* is equipped with the usual niches for clothing as well as a cold plunge; and off it open the *tepi-*

Lararium with a painting of Vesta and scenes in a bakery

The Stabian Baths: reconstruction

darium and the *calidarium*, the latter also equipped with a plunge, and both corresponding closely in other respects to those of the male section. Some of the rooms of this group are decorated in beautiful stuccowork: coffering, fantasy architecture and figures, some white, some coloured, and all dating from the last years of the city's life. To this period belongs also the organisation of the rooms along the west side of the palaestra, including a large open-air pool and a series of changing-rooms. Here the athletes anointed themselves with oil and sand before exercising, afterwards scraping off the sweat and dust with a strigil.

28 VIA DELL'ABBONDANZA

The stretch of the lower decumanus that runs from the Forum to the Sarno Gate takes the name of Via dell'Abbondanza from a relief which adorns a public fountain near the Forum end and which has been thought to represent the goddess of Abundance. It was probably the principal artery of the city, like the other *decumanus,* the Via di Nola, running the whole length of it and connecting all the principal centres: the Forum, the Stabian Baths, the Theatre quarter and the temple of Isis, and finally the Amphitheatre and the great Palaestra. It is also the part of the excavations which comes to life most readily for the visitor, thanks to the up-to-date methods of its excavation and conservation. Greater attention to the surviving superstructures and a better technique of restoration have made possible the recomposition and consolidation of whatever came from the upper storeys.

The result has been to acquire much new and often quite unexpected knowledge about this particular aspect of ancient architecture (upper storeys with terraces and small porticoes, often bracketed out from the facade below) and in many respects also to change traditional beliefs about the Roman atrium house. Another innovation has been to leave all objects where they were found, so that one can now see in place, painted in large

The Stabian Baths:
stucco work with Ganymede and the eagle

Via dell'Abbondanza: reconstruction

red letters on the stucco of the house facades, the electoral posters, and beside them innumerable smaller painted or scratched texts, verses and poems, imprecations, lampoons and obscenities. The main shops hang out their signs to attract custom, and laid out on the counters and shelves are glasses, terracottas and bronzes. The workshops of the artisans contain the tools and equipment of their craft, and from the surviving decoration of the houses and the objects in use we can form an impression of the varying social status of the houses - a variety far greater than one would ever have imagined. The large *House of the Cryptoporticus* is remarkable for its elaborate plan and for the covered gallery which gives it its name, finely decorated in the Second Style and converted into a cellar by its last owner. The nearby *House of Paquius Proculus* on the other hand has preserved its handsome atrium with a figured mosaic pavement and its spacious peristyle. Across the street the *House of the Moralist,* with its painted epigrams in the dining-room, offers a glimpse of Pompeian society behaviour, while the *Thermopolium* (Bar) *delle Aselline* embodies the less polished manners of the tavern world. As one moves away from the centre towards the *Porta di Sarno* the houses grow less and less urban in character, both in lay-out and in the proportion of open space, approximating increasingly to the suburban villas. Past the *House of the Venus*, the *House of Octavius Quartio* and the *Villa of Julia Felix*, one passes in almost logical sequence out into the open countryside beyond the walls, out into the ever-fertile *Ager Pompeianus.*

29 THE HOUSE OF D. OCTAVIUS QUARTIO (REG. II)

The door with its great bronze nails is based on a plaster cast; the atrium is plain and the impluvium has become a flower bed. The best part of the house is the peristyle and the annexed pergola-covered loggia; the paintings of Pyramus and Thisbe and of Narcissus in the triclinium at the far end, though unpretentious, are unusual because at the time of their excavation the signature of the *Lucius pinxit* could be read. On the wall of one large hall are two bands of fine painted scenes from the story of Hercules and the Trojan cycle, and included among the elegant Fourth Style paintings of a small room opening off the west side of it is a figure of a priest of Isis, which is perhaps a portrait of one of the house's occupants.

Below the loggia, in the large garden (*hortus*) beyond, runs a small channel (*euripus*) with miniature cascades, a tank with a fountain and a tempietto; along the edge are ornamental statuettes, animals, muses, marble herms, and along on either side of it ran paths shaded by pergolas. All of these

The House of D. Octavius Quartio:
the pergola above the garden

elements are typical of the great villas, of which this 'little villa in the city' offers a miniature reproduction.

30 THE HOUSE OF THE VENUS (REG. II)

This is another of the Pompeian houses which at the time of the eruption had not yet completely recovered from the earthquake. This is particularly clear in the mosaic-paved dining-room, of which the walls are merely plastered in readiness for the customary painted decoration.

The main rooms are disposed along the wings of the garden. On two sides of this are porticoes, the columns stuccoed and painted in golden yellow and white, while the rear wall is painted with a scheme that reflects its setting, depicting a hedge with flowering shrubs, marble basins with doves drinking from them and a statue of Mars on a base. The subject of the central scene is quite different, representing Venus skimming the ocean, reclining in a cockle-shell with two attendant cupids. The merits of the picture lie in its lively colour and decorative qualities rather than its artistry, and it offers a vivid illustration of the capacities and limitations of the local artists in interpreting and reelaborating the familiar mythological subjects which they inherited from other and abler hands.

House of the Venus: painting of a statue of Mars

Venus in the cockle shell

The Villa of Julia Felix: scenes of life in the Forum

31 THE VILLA OF JULIA FELIX (REG. II)

This is a large residence, laid out on an unusual plan. A door from the Via dell'Abbondanza, painted with scenes showing life in the Forum, leads through a large vestibule into the portico around the garden. This has slender, elegant marble pilasters and off it open a series of rooms, notably a triclinium with marble-façade couches and in the rear wall an aedicula, which emitted a cascade of water into a channel beneath. In the south side there is a shrine, perhaps for the cult of Isis.

At the far end are the living quarters, with service rooms round an atrium and an entrance from the alley to the west. The garden forms an elongated rectangle, with pilasters, probably for a pergola, on the other two sides and a fish-pool down the centre, with miniature bridges and marble niches. A separate en-

The Villa of Julia Felix: reconstruction

The Villa of Julia Felix: still-life paintings

trance from the Via dell'Abbondanza leads to the *balneum*. This is a small, well designed bath-building which, as we learn from an inscription (which gives the owner's name) was built and rented out for public use. It includes a small porticoed courtyard, a changing-room with a cold plunge, a *tepidarium*, a *calidarium* and a circular *laconicum* for *sudationes* (dry sweating); also an open air pool, furnace and latrine. Alongside the villa is a large orchard, and fronting on to the street a tavern and row of two-storeyed shops, which must also have been rented out.

The Villa, excavated and reburied in the mid-18th century, was again uncovered in 1952-53. Some of the rich decoration in marble, painting and sculpture was dispersed by the original excavators (some

The Amphitheatre

paintings showing Apollo and the Muses are now in the Louvre, and others are in Naples Museum), but finds in the recent excavation included a terracotta statuette of Pittacus of Mytilene.

32 THE AMPHITHEATRE

The oldest known Roman amphitheatre. It was erected about 80 B.C. under the duoviri C. Quintius Valgus and M. Porcius, who also built the Little Theatre. The arena is at a lower level than the surrounding ground, so that the building is partly sunk and lacks substructures. The seats were reached by external staircases. These are substantial remains of the seating, as well as of the upper gallery, reserved for women. Inside the building was decorated with paintings representing the various games that took place in the amphiteatre. It constitutes a valuable document for the early development of a type of monument which was

Battle between the Pompeians and their neighbours of Nocera. From the outside wall of House I.3.23 (National Museum of Naples)

House of Menander:
detail of a Cupid on a grape-vine

very popular in Roman times, and which was subsequently developed and elaborated in the great amphitheatres of the Imperial age. The seating was shaded by a *velarium* (canopy) supported by poles, as we learn from the programmes of the games and as can be seen in the famous painting (kept in the Naples Museum) showing the riot that explosed between the inhabitants of Pompeii and Nuceria in the year 59 A.D. The restorations undertaken after the earthquake were probably the work of the duoviri C. Cuspius Pansa and his son.

33 THE PALAESTRA

Alongside is a huge palaestra, with an enclosing wall and porticoes on three sides. The swimming pool in the centre was surrounded by a double row of plane-trees.

34 THE HOUSE OF THE MENANDER (REG. I)

Like the House of the Golden Cupids this belonged to a branch of the influential family of the *Poppaei*. The entrance is flanked by two dignified pilasters with Corinthian capitals. Within the Tuscan atrium, decorated in the Fourth Style, is the Lararium and in one of the rooms opening off it a series of small panels depicting episodes from the Trojan cycle: Laocoon, the Trojan Horse, Cassandra. Beyond the *tablinum* lie the fine columnar peristyle and a series of rooms, one of which has an elegant decorative scheme on a green background with cupids among vineshoots and a mosaic pavement containing a Nilotic panel; another, a large dining-room, incorporates at a lower level earlier structures decorated in the Second Style. An exedra at the back has paintings showing in the center Diana inside a small temple. Another exedra has theatrical paintings including a portrait of the poet Menander, whence the name of the house. Along one side lies the bath-suite, elegantly decorated with paintings and mosaics; off the other lie the domestic quarters. In the basement was found a silver service of 115 pieces, now in the Naples Museum.

House of the Menander: portrait of the poet

The Temple of Isis

35 THE TEMPLE OF ISIS (REG. VIII)

The sanctuary of an Egyptian cult that attained great popularity in the Roman world, it was first built during the IInd century B.C. and was completely rebuilt after the earthquake of 62 through the generosity of Numerius Popidius Celsinus. It is the most complete of the city's temples. Building, decoration and sacred furnishings were all perfectly preserved, when found (1764-1766). Paintings and sculptures are now in a room of Naples Museum which reconstructs and respects as much as possible the original aspect of the decoration. The precinct is surrounded by a high wall, with a single entrance so situated that from the street nothing could be seen of the ceremonies conducted within the enclosure. The small temple stands on a tall podium and consists of a porch and a cella, within which were the sacred objects characteristic of the Isiac cult. Below, near the steps, is the altar; at the south-east corner of the court there is a roofless enclosure from where one descended into an underground cavity in which was kept the sacred Nile water; and on the other side a covered enclosure served as a repository for the ashes and remains of sacrifices. Behind the temple there is a large hall which was built on an area which originally belonged to the neighbouring Samnite palaestra.

36 THE TRIANGULAR FORUM (REG. VIII)

The Triangular Forum, which took its shape from the stretch of level ground in which it was built, is another centre that was linked with buildings of a public character. Flanked internally by two Doric porticoes, raised during the Samnite period and which stood a Doric temple of the mid 6th century B.C. thought to associate the cult of Athena with that of Hercules. Partly destroyed in the Samnite period, only the basis and scanty fragments of the superstructure survive, including architectural terracottas. In Roman times it was reduced to a mere shrine. Other features of the Forum were a statue of Marcellus, August's nephew, three Samnite-period tufa altars, a circular aedicula with a well, and a semicircular seat (*exedra*) with a sundial.

From the east portico of the forum a door gave access to a palaestra also built in the Samnite period, in which was found a copy of the Doryphoros of Polycleitos; and another door led to the *summa*

The Temple of Isis: the arrival of Io in Egypt

Sacred scene

cavea of the Large Theatre. There was access also, by means of a broad flight of steps, to the spacious portico enclosure which lies behind the stage-building of the theatre.

37 THE THEATRE (REG. VIII)

Pompeii had two theatres, a smaller, roofed Odeon for recitations, musical performances and mimes, and a larger theatre which was open but could if necessary be covered with an awning. In its present form the latter dates from a restoration of the 1st century A.D.

The upper zone of seating (*summa cavea*) is raised on a vaulted corridor (*crypta*), the middle and lower zones rest on the ground, with the *tribunalia* for distinguished spectators set over the entrances to the orchestra. It held about 5000 spectators. The orchestra, no longer used by actors and chorus, was also available for seating, probably for citizens of the upper classes. There was a low stage of Roman type, the rear wall of which was carried up in an elaborate scheme of recesses and *aediculae*, with three doors to simulate the façade of a palace. Behind it lay a room used by the actors, and beyond this again a rec-

The Triangular Forum: detail of the portico

Doric Temple

tangular space enclosed by porticoes. This was the *porticus post scaenam* (**38**) used by the spectators in the intervals or in bad weather. The name of the architect of the theatre in this, its latest, form is known - M. Artorius Primus, a contemporary of Augustus.

There had been earlier structural phases. The original building, was built in the IInd century B.C. within the context of the urban development of this part of the city, following a Hellenistic model, had limestone tiers which followed for the greater part the natural slope of the hillside and was smaller than the present one. Some structural alterations can be dated towards the beginning of the 1st century B.C., whereas the enlarging of the *cavea*, the seating for the spectators, can be attributed to the period of Augustus and was obtained with the construction of an elevated upper zone, *summa cavea*, over the crypt and held up by the arches and pilasters, and the marble covering of the steps, and the remodelling of the *tribunalia*. The *scaena frons* (the "back-cloth") maybe could be of a period subsequent to the earthquake of 62 A.D. For the work of M. Artorius Primus, mentioned above, and for the munificence of the two distinguished citizens, M. Holconius Rufus and M. Holconius Celer, who paid for it, we have a group of inscriptions found in the theatre.

The *velarium* (awning) that gave shade to the building, was held up by pilasters which are inserted in the *summa cavea* and was stretched and adjusted as required by means of a system of ropes and pulleys. The *velarium* that covered the *frons scaenae* worked in a similar way.

L'Odeon

39 THE ODEON (REG. VIII)

The Small Theatre, or Odeon, held about 1000 spectators and was intended for more intimate programmes such as concerts, recitations of verses and mimes. It was built about the year 80 B.C. by the duoviri C. Quintius Valgus and M. Porcius. Unlike the Large Theatre it had a permanent timber roof, probably with four slopes. There are only two zones of seating, the upper one of which was separated from the lower by a balustrade and the seats are almost completely preserved; a pair of *telamon* figures carved in tufa mark the ends of the parapets on either side.

The Theatre: reconstruction

The paving of the orchestra, furnished by the duovir M. Oculatius Verus, was of marble, as must also have been the facing of the stage.

The remodelling of the balustrade and the construction of the tribunalia can probably be ascribed to a modification carried out during the period of Augustus. For the rest the building maintained the original balance of its plan, structure and ornament. The result is an unusually harmonious example of late Hellenistic taste and one which constitutes an important landmark in the architectural history of Pompeii.

The Villas of the Mysteries: Fresco. Fleeing girl

THE SUBURBAN VILLAS

40 THE VILLA OF THE MYSTERIES

The finest example of a suburban villa, renowned alike for its size and its many wall-paintings, notably those of the dining-room from which the villa takes its name. Not yet completely cleared, it stands a short distance outside the town beyond the Herculaneum Gate and was entered from a street which presumably connected with the Via delle Tombe. Between the entrance and the peristyle lies the domestic wing with a kitchen, a bakery with its oven, the *prelum* for pressing the grapes, the wine cellar and the slaves' quarters. The domestic wing (through which one now enters) is disposed about a tablinum and atrium, which a decoration reproducing a marble-slab lining, which opens off the peristyle, also decorated in the same way. The nucleus of the villa goes back to the 2nd century B.C., but it later underwent several enlargements and restorations, enjoying a period of brilliance as a patrician villa and then as Imperial property. In its last years it passed to the family of the Istacidii who converted it into a villa rustica.

The great frieze that occupies the walls of the dining-room is the work of a Campanian artist of the 1st century B.C. under the influence of Greek painting. There is considerable dispute among scholars about the exact significance of these paintings, but there seems to be no doubt that they are in some way related to the mystery cults, and they are usually thought to represent the successive stages of a wife's initiation into the mysteries of Dionysus.

Starting with the north wall and reading from left to right, the cycle begins with a child, guided by a seated matron, reading from a papyrus the regulations for the sacred rites. There follows a scene of offerings and sacrifice, and a pastoral scene with a Silen playing the lyre; and at the end of the wall, a woman starting back in terror. In the middle of east wall the marriage of Dionysus and Ariadne symbolises the happiness that awaits the initiated in the after-world; on the left a Silen and two Satyrs, and on the right a woman unveiling the symbol of fertility and a winged figure raising a scourge. Next comes a woman being scourged, who hides her face in the lap of a companion, followed by a nude, dancing Bacchante. To complete the cycle there are two portraits of the matron, one completing her toilet, the other seated and mantled, already initiated and the mystic bride of the god. Both in content and in quality these paintings are among the finest preserved from antiquity.

Neighbouring the dining-room there is a cubicle with two alcoves with red background decorations, of which also the upper part is well conserved.

41 THE VILLA OF DIOMEDE

The discovery of this villa in 1771-74 made a great impression on the archaeological and literary world, not least because of the finding of eighteen bodies in the underground portico. Unfortunately, except for some paintings in Naples Museum, little survives on the spot of the rich decoration which

The Villa of Diomede:
reconstruction

marked it out as an upper-class residence. After the Villa of the Mysteries it is the most important suburban building yet excavated.

A discrete but tasteful entrance, set within a small portico, leads from the Via delle Tombe into the Peristyle. A triangular area on the east side houses the baths, with a small portico and a pool for bathing. The dwelling rooms lie to the north and south and include a room with three windows and an apse, preceded by an anteroom. From the same side one passes through the tablinum, which was later enlarged by the construction of a large room built partly over the portico beneath; thence to other rooms and to a second terrace which runs right round the garden, serving as an *ambulatio* and *solarium*, for exercise and sunshine. A ramp and staircase led down to the spacious square garden, in the middle of which were a large pool and a summer dining-room surrounded by columns.Round it ran a portico with windows (later closed) facing outwards and two belvedere turrets at the angles of the side towards the sea. Two small flights of steps led down into the cryptoportico, lit by small splay-windows facing inwards and outwards; it was also used as a cellar. The position is a fine one, and the villa was obviously laid out so that both the terrace and the dwelling rooms should make the best use both of the view and of the sunshine.

Antiquarium.
Casts of the eruption's victims

THE ANTIQUARIUM

This offers a broad documentation of the history and art of Pompeii through a display of typical finds. In the entrance, wall-maps illustrating the progress of the excavation from 1748 to 1948.

In Room I, the protohistory of the Sarno Valley (9th-8th century B.C.); architectural terracottas from the Doric Temple and the Temple of Apollo (6th-5th century B.C.); fragments of Greek pottery and archaic Etruscan bucchero. In Room II, sculpture of the Samnite period (3rd-

2nd century B.C.); the sphinx from the fondo Barbatelli, composite capitals with figures of Maenads and Satyrs; metope with the punishment of Ixion; pediment of the Dionysiac shrine outside the city, with Dionysus and Ariadne. In the next room, Roman portraits: Livia, wife of Augustus, and Marcellus, his nephew; Cornelius Rufus, Vesonius Primus, Suedius Clemens and other Pompeian worthies. Finally, two rooms in which are displayed remains illustrating the daily life of Pompeii: bronze forniture, jewellery, wall-paintings, small decorative sculpture of the Roman period; also plaster casts of bodies and of other objects, and a small-scale model of the Boscoreale villa rustica.

The Villa of Mysteries: the atrium

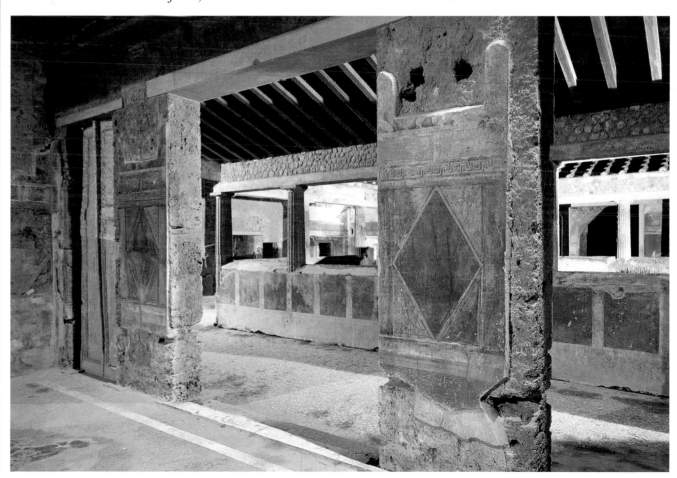

CONTENTS

3 Pompei, its life and history
9 Porta Marina and Villa Suburbana
9 Temple of Venus
10 The Forum
10 The Forum and the Capitolium
12 The Temple of Apollo
14 The Basilica
16 Buildings of the Forum
18 The Temple of Fortuna Augusta
18 The Forum Baths
20 The House of the Tragic Poet
21 The House of Sallust
21 The Herculaneum Gate
22 The Street of the Tombs
24 The House of Meleager
25 The House of the Large Fountain
25 The House of the Faun
26 The House of the Vettii
29 The House of the Golden Cupids
30 The House of L. Caecilius Jucundus
30 The House of the Silver Wedding
31 The House of the Centenary
31 The Central Baths
32 Pistrinum (Bakery)
34 The Stabian Baths
36 Via dell'Abbondanza
38 The House of D. Octavius Quartio
39 The House of the Venus
40 The Villa of Julia Felix
43 The Amphitheatre
44 The House of the Menander
45 The Temple of Isis
46 The Triangular Forum
47 The Theatre
48 The Odeon
51 The Villa of the Mysteries
52 The Villa of Diomede
54 Antiquarium